Early TOY Encyclopedias

BARBIE

by Laura Stickney

Early Encyclopedias

An Imprint of Abdo Reference

abdobooks.com

abdobooks.com

Published by Abdo Reference, a division of ABDO, PO Box 398166, Minneapolis, Minnesota 55439.

Printed in China.
052025
092025

THIS BOOK CONTAINS RECYCLED MATERIALS

Editor: Haley Williams
Series Designers: Candice Keimig, Joshua Olson
Production Designer: Ryan Gale

Library of Congress Control Number: 2024949032

Publisher's Cataloging-in-Publication Data

Names: Stickney, Laura, author.
Title: Barbie / by Laura Stickney
Description: Minneapolis, Minnesota: Abdo Reference, 2026 | Series: Early toy encyclopedias | Includes online resources and index.
Identifiers: ISBN 9781098297541 (lib. bdg.) | ISBN 9798384930068 (ebook)
Subjects: LCSH: Barbie dolls--Juvenile literature. | Dolls--Juvenile literature. | Toys--Juvenile literature. | Popular culture--Juvenile literature. | Collectibles--Juvenile literature. | Reference materials--Juvenile literature. | Encyclopedias and dictionaries--Juvenile literature.
Classification: DDC 688.722--dc23

CONTENTS

INTRODUCTION

Some people enjoy collecting new and old Barbie dolls.

An Iconic Toy

Barbie is the most popular fashion doll in history. Most Barbie dolls have movable plastic arms and legs. They have lifelike hair. People can buy accessories for the dolls. These include clothing, dollhouses, and cars. Boys and girls of all ages enjoy playing with Barbies.

No. 1 Fashion Doll

Barbie has become a major toy brand. The dolls are sold in 150 countries. More than 100 dolls are sold per minute. Many Barbie toys hit the shelves every year. Barbie is also one of the most diverse doll brands.

Toy stores often have sections just for Barbie dolls and playsets.

INTRODUCTION

Birth of Barbie

Barbie was invented by Ruth Handler. In 1945, Handler, her husband, and businessman Harold Matson started a toy company. They called it Mattel. Most dolls at that time were baby dolls. Handler's daughter, Barbara, also played with paper dolls. Handler realized that girls did not have as many toy options as boys.

Ruth Handler, *left*, and her husband, Elliot, *right*, sold a variety of toys in Mattel's early days, including toy furniture and pianos.

Barbie's Debut

Handler decided to make a three-dimensional version of paper dolls. On March 9, 1959, she debuted Barbie at a toy fair in New York City. Handler named the doll after her daughter.

FUN FACT!

Barbie was inspired by the German doll Bild Lilli.

Barbie dolls quickly became popular toys.

Barbie World

Many people thought Barbie was inappropriate for kids. They did not like that the doll had an adult woman's figure. But that did not stop Barbie from becoming popular. More than 300,000 Barbies were sold in the first year.

First Commercial

The first Barbie commercial aired in 1959. It appeared during a children's TV show. A song in the ad helped make Barbies popular.

Fans and Critics

Barbie quickly became a best-selling toy. Some people praised the doll. They thought it challenged traditional ideas about women. With Barbies, girls could imagine different careers and futures for themselves. But others thought the doll promoted unrealistic beauty standards.

The first Barbie career doll, *left*, was a fashion designer. The doll was released in 1960.

FUN FACT!

Ruth Handler named the Ken doll after her son, Kenneth.

Barbie Expands

More Barbie toys came out during the 1960s and 1970s. In 1961, Mattel introduced Ken. He was the first male Barbie doll. Mattel later sold Barbies with new careers. These dolls had careers that many people believed only men could have.

Barbie dolls were originally marketed only to girls.

The look and design of Barbies have changed a lot since 1959.

Making Barbie Inclusive

In 1968, Mattel released its first Black doll. Her name was Christie. The first Black and Hispanic dolls named Barbie came out in 1980. The 1990s saw the release of the first Barbie in a wheelchair. The Dolls of the World series featured dolls from different countries.

More than 100 dolls have released under the Fashionistas line.

Barbie Today

The Barbie brand grew in the 2000s. The Fashionistas line debuted in 2009. Barbies and Kens with different body types were eventually added to the line. The dolls had diverse hairstyles and skin tones. Fashionistas also featured dolls with disabilities and skin conditions.

Barbie on the Big Screen

In 2023, the Barbie brand grew in popularity. This was due to the hit film *Barbie*. The movie became a pop culture sensation. Mattel created many dolls and toy sets based on the movie. Barbie toy sales grew. This showed that Barbies would remain a popular toy.

Barbie Toy Sales

Since 2019, Barbie toy sales have risen in North America.

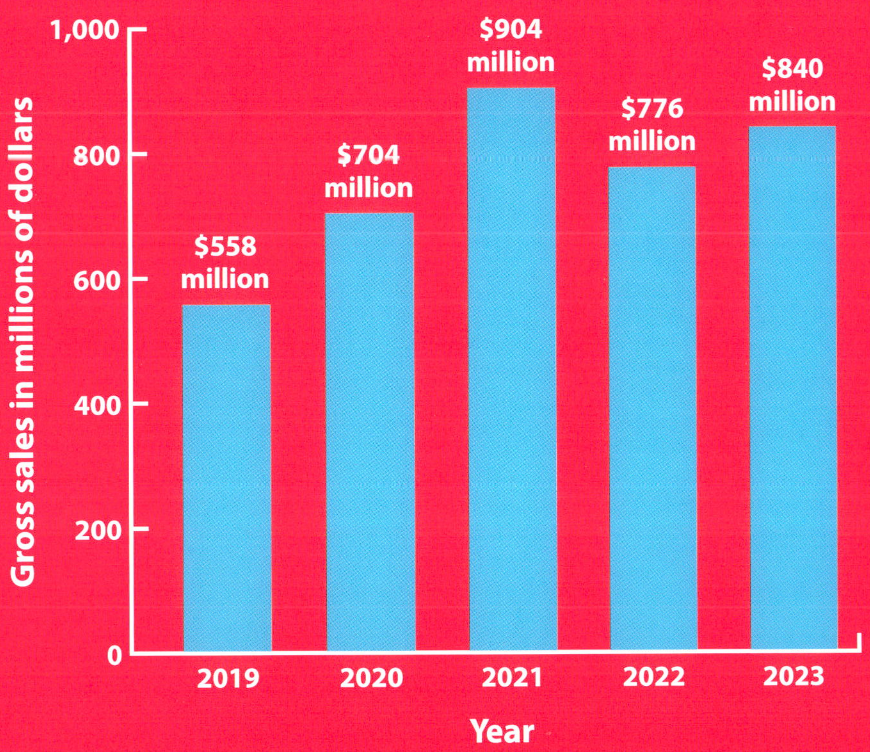

No. 1 Barbie

The first Barbie doll was called Teenage Fashion Model Barbie. The doll came with a black-and-white striped swimsuit. She wore white sunglasses. She had black shoes. And her hair was in a ponytail. Today, many people call this doll No. 1 Barbie.

The first Barbie doll was supposed to be 19 years old.

FUN FACT!

Barbie's full name is Barbara Millicent Roberts.

Style Icon

No. 1 Barbie had red lips and arched eyebrows. Her eyes looked sideways. And her nails were painted red. These features were based on those of movie stars in the 1950s. People could buy dolls with blonde or brown hair.

Dresses and skirts were common clothing sold for early Barbie dolls.

The Miss Astronaut space suit was based on those worn by real astronauts during the 1960s.

The 1960s

In the 1960s, Mattel updated Barbie's features. She could come with red hair. The company also designed Barbies with different careers. These included a flight attendant and nurse. In 1965, the Miss Astronaut set was released. It came with a silver space suit and helmet.

New Features

Soon after, Mattel began making Barbies with bendable legs. One was Color Magic Barbie. She came out in 1966. This doll's outfit and hair changed color. People used a liquid to change the colors. One year later, Twiggy Barbie came out. She was based on the British model Twiggy.

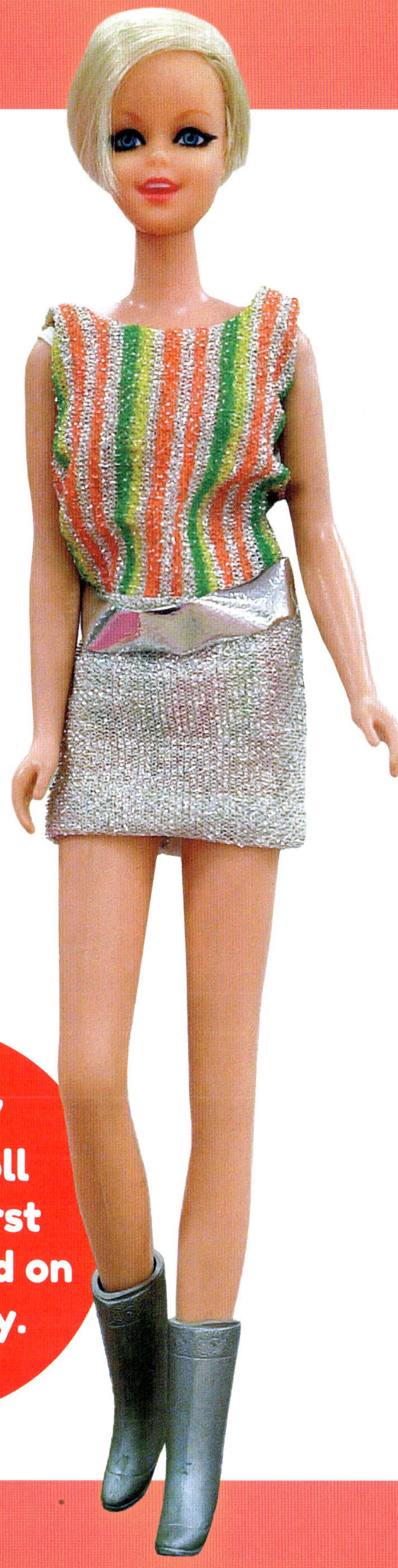

The 1967 Twiggy doll was the first Barbie based on a celebrity.

The 1970s

In the 1970s, Mattel released Barbies inspired by popular styles. Malibu Barbie hit the shelves in 1971. This was the first Barbie whose eyes looked forward. The doll was a California surfer girl. She had blonde hair and tanned skin. She wore a blue swimsuit and purple sunglasses.

Malibu Barbie came with a beach towel.

When Doctor Barbie came out in 1973, few women had careers as doctors.

More Careers

Opportunities for women were growing during the 1970s. Barbies reflected these changes. Mattel released new career dolls. One was Doctor Barbie. She came out in 1973. She wore medical scrubs. Accessories included a face mask and medical bag.

First Black Barbie

Early Barbie dolls were almost all white. Before 1980, the only Black dolls were sold as Barbie's friends. Designer Kitty Black Perkins joined Mattel in 1976. She created the first Black doll named Barbie. It came out in 1980. The doll wore a red dress. She had curly hair.

Designer Kitty Black Perkins wanted to make sure her doll reflected the looks of Black women.

Kitty Black Perkins

Kitty Black Perkins was Mattel's first Black designer. She went on to become the chief designer for Barbie. Black Perkins designed many dolls during her career.

First Hispanic Barbie

In 1980, Mattel released the first Hispanic Barbie. She had dark eyes. She also had long dark hair. The doll wore a white blouse and red skirt. The box included English and Spanish text. Mattel began making more diverse dolls after that.

Hispanic Barbie had a red flower necklace, ring, and earrings.

More than 100 Barbies have been released in the Dolls of the World collection.

Dolls of the World

In 1980, Mattel began its Dolls of the World line. These dolls represented different countries. Kids could read about the country on the doll's box. Each doll wore a traditional outfit from its country.

FUN FACT!

Dolls of the World was one of the longest-running Barbie series.

1980–1989

Several Dolls of the World came out in the 1980s. The 1982 India Barbie wore a red-and-gold sari. The 1986 Peruvian Barbie had braids and a colorful skirt. Other dolls in the collection included Spanish Barbie, Irish Barbie, and Japanese Barbie.

Mexican Barbie was released in 1989.

1990–1999

Dolls of the World continued into the 1990s. Nigerian Barbie, Jamaican Barbie, and Australian Barbie were added to the series. Four versions of Native American Barbie also came out. The first was released in 1993. Mattel made second editions of some dolls as well.

The second version of Native American Barbie came out in 1994.

Limited Edition

In 1994, Mattel released two limited edition sets. Each came with three Dolls of the World. One had Chinese Barbie, Dutch Barbie, and Kenyan Barbie. The other had Irish Barbie, German Barbie, and Polynesian Barbie. Another gift set released in 1995. It had Japanese Barbie, Norwegian Barbie, and Indian Barbie.

Many of the Dolls of the World Barbies were either special editions or collector's items.

Princess Collection

In 2000, Mattel started the Princess Collection. The dolls represented princesses from different countries and cultures. Princess of Ancient Mexico Barbie wore a feather headdress. Princess of the Navajo Barbie had a woven shawl.

Princess Collection Timeline

Between 2000 and 2005, Mattel released 21 dolls in the Princess Collection.

2000
- Princess of the French Court
- Princess of India

2001
- Princess of Ancient Mexico
- Princess of China
- Princess of Ireland
- Princess of the Incas
- Princess of the Nile

2002
- Princess of South Africa
- Princess of the Danish Court
- Princess of the Portuguese Empire

2003
- Princess of Ancient Greece
- Princess of Cambodia
- Princess of England
- Princess of Japan
- Princess of the Vikings

2004
- Princess of Imperial Russia
- Princess of the Korean Court
- Princess of the Navajo
- Princess of the Renaissance

2005
- Princess of Holland
- Princess of the Pacific Islands

Festivals and Landmark Collections

In 2006, Mattel introduced the Festivals of the World line. The dolls represented festivals around the globe. One was Chinese New Year Barbie. In 2010, the Landmark Collection launched. Barbies had clothes inspired by famous landmarks. This included the Statue of Liberty.

Day-to-Night Barbie

Day-to-Night Barbie, *middle*, worked as a chief executive officer.

Mattel released Day-to-Night Barbie in 1985. This doll represented working women. She had outfits for both day and night. The doll wore a pink business suit. She carried a briefcase. Her suit could turn into a party dress.

Barbie in Space

In 1986, a second Astronaut Barbie came out. She had a shiny space suit. It was hot pink and silver. The doll also came with a space helmet. Several other astronaut Barbies were released in the 1990s. These dolls had more realistic space suits.

The space suit for the 1986 Astronaut Barbie had puffy sleeves inspired by 1980s fashions.

Each Teen Talk Barbie said four recorded phrases.

The 1990s

During the 1990s, Mattel released many popular Barbies. Some new dolls had special features. One was the 1992 Teen Talk Barbie. Kids could press a button on the doll's back. This made the Barbie say recorded phrases.

A Problematic Phrase

Many people criticized Teen Talk Barbie. They didn't like that she said, "Math class is tough!" Mattel removed the phrase from the dolls in late 1992.

Bestseller

In 1992, Mattel released the best-selling Barbie of all time. It was Totally Hair Barbie. This doll had ankle-length hair. She came with hair gel and hair accessories. Kids could style the doll's hair. Mattel sold more than ten million Totally Hair Barbies.

Mattel rereleased Totally Hair Barbie in 2017.

Barbie for President

Mattel released President Barbie in 1992. She wore a red-and-blue ball gown. The doll also came with a red suit. In 2000, a second President Barbie came out. The doll wore a blue suit and a campaign button. She came with campaign stickers and signs.

The 1992 President Barbie came with a button that said, "Barbie for President."

The only year between 1992 and 2020 that Barbie did not run for president was 1996.

Running for Office

More President Barbies were created throughout the 2000s. The 2004 President Barbie wore a red pantsuit. In 2008 and 2012, President Barbie wore a skirt. In 2016, Mattel released a two-doll set. It came with a president and vice president.

Barbie has had more than 250 careers.

I Can Be . . .

In 2009, another Barbie line hit the shelves. It was called Barbie I Can Be. This series featured dolls with a variety of careers. These included a vet, race car driver, and gymnastics coach. Each doll had accessories related to her job.

Career of the Year

In 2010, Mattel introduced its Career of the Year series. Each year, it picked a career to feature. Then it released a Barbie who represented that career. The first doll was Computer Engineer Barbie. Other Careers of the Year have included a game developer and judge.

Computer Engineer Barbie came with a laptop and cell phone.

Sheroes

Mattel began its Barbie Sheroes line in 2015. It honored inspiring women. The dolls were designed to look like each Shero. The first line included seven dolls. Filmmaker Ava DuVernay and actress Zendaya were among those honored.

A Shero doll of US Olympic fencer Ibtihaj Muhammad was made in 2017.

FUN FACT!

The name *Sheroes* is a combination of the words *she* and *heroes.*

Role Models

Mattel releases new Sheroes every year. The collection has featured actresses and athletes. It has featured activists and artists. The 2016 line included ballerina Misty Copeland. YouTube chief executive officer Susan Wojcicki was honored in 2023.

Misty Copeland was the first Black female principal dancer at the American Ballet Theatre.

Fashionistas dolls come with a variety of hair colors, including purple, blue, and multicolored.

Fashionistas

In the mid-2010s, Mattel updated its Barbie Fashionistas line. The dolls had more modern fashions. In 2015, Mattel added new dolls to the line. It offered seven skin colors and 22 eye colors. There were also 24 different hairstyles.

Inclusive Dolls

The Fashionistas line included dolls with different body types. Some were tall, curvy, or petite. Mattel hoped these dolls would help represent all kids. In 2019, the company introduced dolls with disabilities. One doll was in a wheelchair. Another had a prosthetic limb.

Mattel has released both Barbie and Ken dolls with prosthetic legs.

Fashionistas Expands

In 2020, more dolls joined the Fashionistas line. One Barbie had vitiligo. This is a skin condition. Another Barbie had no hair. She represented people who experience hair loss. In 2022, Mattel introduced dolls with hearing aids.

The Barbie with no hair comes with a brightly colored dress and gold hoop earrings.

Mattel continues working to make Barbie inclusive for people of all backgrounds.

More Milestones

In 2023, Mattel released the first Barbie with Down syndrome. The company made sure the condition was accurately represented. Mattel added a Black Barbie with Down syndrome the next year. It also released a blind Barbie. This doll came with a cane. She had textured clothing. This made the toy accessible for people with blindness.

Astronaut Sally Ride and mathematician Katherine Johnson are among the people honored in the Inspiring Women line.

Inspiring Women

In 2018, Mattel started its Inspiring Women line. This was like the Barbie Sheroes series. But it featured historical role models. Early dolls included pilot Amelia Earhart and artist Frida Kahlo.

Historical Heroes

Mattel designed many Inspiring Women dolls. They were released throughout the 2010s and 2020s. Featured women included author Maya Angelou and activist Wilma Mankiller. Animal researcher Jane Goodall and tennis star Billie Jean King were also honored.

A doll of historical figure Helen Keller was released in 2021.

National Geographic Barbies

In 2019, the Barbie brand partnered with National Geographic. This organization focuses on science and wildlife. It helped Mattel design a Barbie line. One doll was a polar marine biologist. Another was a wildlife reporter. Playsets were included with each doll.

Five Barbie dolls came out under the National Geographic line.

The Barbie Loves the Ocean dolls, accessories, and sets were made from 90 percent recycled plastic.

Going Green

In the 2020s, Mattel set a goal. The company planned to use more recycled plastics in its products. In 2021, Mattel released Barbie Loves the Ocean. This line featured the first Barbies made from recycled plastic. The dolls' outfits were also made from recycled materials.

At the beginning of the *Barbie* movie, Margot Robbie is dressed as the No. 1 Barbie.

Barbie Movie

In 2023, the live-action film *Barbie* came out. Margot Robbie plays Barbie. In the movie, Barbie lives a perfect life in Barbieland. Then she and Ken travel into the real world. Barbie realizes the world is not so perfect. The film explores the roles Barbies have played in peoples' lives.

Popularity Boost

The movie made more people interested in the Barbie brand. Mattel's toy sales grew. The company released several Barbies based on the film. These dolls wore outfits from the movie. One was a pink cowgirl outfit. It came with a white western hat.

The Barbie dolls based on the film were made to look like Margot Robbie.

Barbie Then and Now

Barbies have changed a lot since 1959. Dolls today are more diverse and can move more than the original dolls.

Made to Move

Mattel introduced Barbie Made to Move in the 2020s. These dolls were designed to bend in natural ways. Each doll had 22 joints. Kids could bend the doll's elbows, wrists, and knees. They could put the Barbies in different poses.

Playtime Possibilities

Made to Move dolls provided more possibilities for play. Many of the dolls came in athletic outfits. They could stretch and do yoga poses. Some dolls wore sports gear. One was a basketball player. Others were a boxer and a skateboarder.

Yoga poses were featured on the boxes of the Made to Move dolls.

More Role Models

In 2024, Mattel released more role model dolls. These dolls honored important female athletes. They were meant to highlight different sports careers. Mattel hoped the dolls would encourage girls to be involved in sports.

Barbie has done many sports over the years, including karate, softball, and rock climbing.

Rebeca Andrade was the first female Brazilian gymnast to win an Olympic medal.

Amazing Athletes

Nine athletes were featured in the 2024 collection. They were known for breaking barriers in their sports. One was US tennis star Venus Williams. Another was Spanish Paralympian Susana Rodriguez. Brazilian gymnast Rebeca Andrade was also featured.

A show called *Barbie Dream Besties* released on YouTube in 2024.

Dream Besties

Dream Besties dolls released in 2024. They were shorter than other Barbies. Their heads and eyes were bigger. Each doll came with accessories. These included makeup, headphones, and cell phones. Each doll represented a hobby or dream job. One was the founder of a makeup line.

Cutie Reveal

The Cutie Reveal collection also came out in the 2020s. Dolls were dressed in animal costumes. Inside each doll's box were ten collectible surprises. These included clothes and pets. Kids could also use hot or cold water to change the Barbie's makeup.

Some of the Cutie Reveal animal costumes included a dog, a rabbit, and a deer.

Boyfriend for Barbie

After Barbie debuted, fans wrote to Mattel. They asked for Barbie to have a boyfriend. So Ruth Handler created the Ken doll. He wore sandals and swimming trunks. He carried a beach towel. His hair was made of felt. Fans could buy a Ken with blond or brown hair.

Ken's full name is Kenneth Carson.

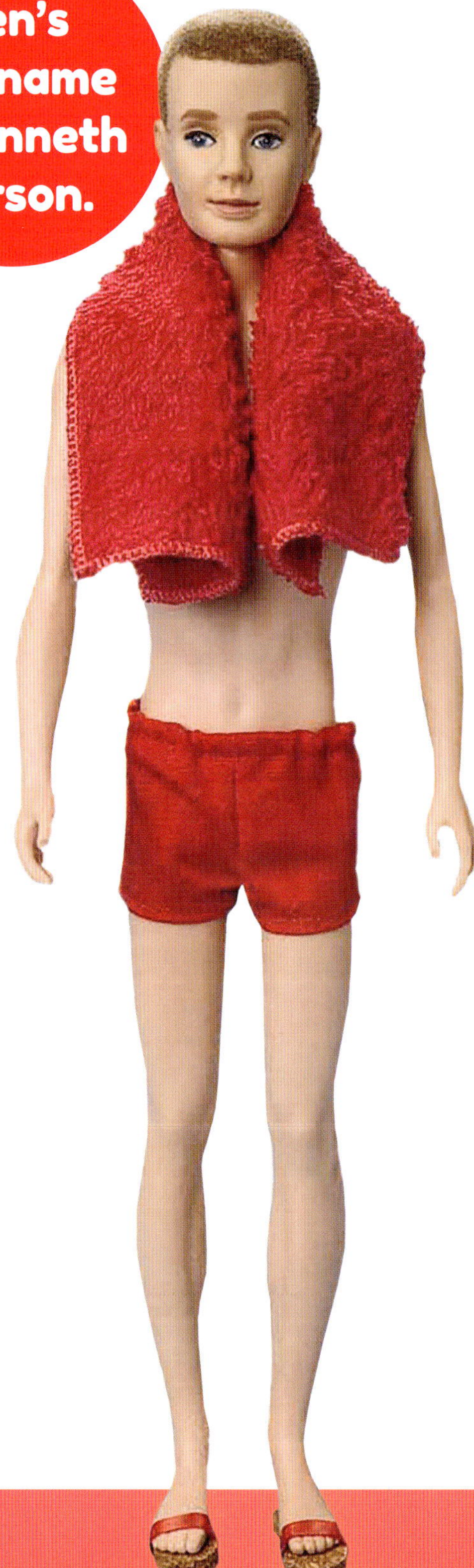

FUN FACT!

Ken is 12 inches (30 cm) tall. He is 0.5 inches (1.3 cm) taller than Barbie.

Ken's birthday is March 11, which is two days after Barbie's.

Ken's Debut

Ken debuted in 1961 at a toy fair. Mattel made an ad about Ken. In the ad, Barbie and Ken meet at a dance. Then they go on dates. Mattel made clothes for Ken. His hair was updated in 1962. It changed to plastic.

Mod Hair Ken was the first Ken to feature more realistic hair that could be brushed.

Ken in the 1970s

In the 1970s, several Kens were released. One was the 1973 Mod Hair Ken. The doll came with stick-on hairpieces. These included a mustache, beard, and sideburns. Superstar Ken came out in 1978. He wore sunglasses and a blue jumpsuit.

Ken Hits the Beach

Sun Lovin' Malibu Ken hit the shelves in 1979. The doll had blond hair and tanned skin. He wore swimming trunks. In 1982, Mattel released the first Black Ken doll. He was called Sunsational Malibu Ken. He had an Afro hairstyle.

The 1982 Sunsational Malibu Ken wore yellow swimming trunks and had blue sunglasses.

Ken in the 1990s

In 1992, Mattel released Totally Hair Ken. The doll had long hair. He came with hair gel. Kids could style the doll's hair. In 1993, Mattel released Earring Magic Ken. He wore a mesh shirt and purple vest. He also had an earring. He became one of the best-selling Kens.

Although Totally Hair Ken released in the 1990s, his clothes were based on styles from the 1970s.

Ken was given a new look in 2006 as a way to help him get back together with Barbie.

New Looks

Shave n' Style Ken came out in 1999. The doll wore jeans and a T-shirt. Facial hair was printed on his face. Kids could dip a toy razor in water to pretend to shave Ken's face. The hair would disappear. Ken dolls got another makeover in 2006. New Look Ken and Beach Fun Ken were among the new dolls.

FUN FACT!

Ken and Barbie broke up in 2004. The dolls started dating again in 2011.

People can buy Fashionista dolls in a store or online.

Ken Joins the Fashionistas

In 2017, Mattel added 15 Kens to its Fashionistas line. The dolls came in seven skin tones. They were available in three body types. The dolls also had a variety of hairstyles. This included cornrows.

More Diverse Kens

Mattel continued to create more diverse Kens. In 2020, a red-haired Ken was added. Two years later, a Ken doll with vitiligo was released. So was a Ken in a wheelchair. Ken dolls with hearing aids and prosthetic limbs have also been added.

Today, Ken and Barbie dolls come in more than 30 skin colors.

He's Just Ken

Ken appeared in the 2023 *Barbie* movie. Ryan Gosling starred as Ken. In the film, Ken is goofy and self-centered. He wears many costumes. He tries to get Barbie's attention. In one scene, he sings a song called "I'm Just Ken." The song became a hit.

I Am Kenough

In the *Barbie* movie, Ken wears a tie-dye sweatshirt. It says "I am Kenough" on it. Mattel made a real version of the sweatshirt. It also made a Ken doll wearing one.

In the *Barbie* movie, Ryan Gosling's Ken and the other Kens take over Barbieland.

Mattel released three Ken dolls and five Barbie dolls based on the 2023 movie.

Burst of Ken-ergy

Gosling's performance went viral. It made people more interested in Ken. Mattel made Ken dolls based on the film. The dolls had outfits inspired by Gosling's character. One Ken had jeans and a denim vest. Another wore a fur coat.

Midge and Allan dolls were not as popular as Barbie and Ken dolls.

First Friends

In 1963, Mattel introduced Midge. She was marketed as Barbie's best friend. The dolls fit into Barbie's clothes. Midge came with red, blonde, or brown hair. In 1964, Allan was released. He was Ken's buddy. He was also Midge's boyfriend. Allan could fit into Ken's clothes.

FUN FACT!

Allan was never popular. Mattel discontinued him after just two years.

Skipper Joins the Family

Mattel released Barbie's first family member in 1964. Her name was Skipper. She was Barbie's little sister. The Skipper doll was shorter than Barbie. She had long hair with bangs. She wore a red swimsuit.

Skipper came with brown, blonde, or red hair.

Christie Makes History

In 1968, Mattel introduced Talking Christie. She was the company's first Black doll. Christie had eyelashes and curly hair. Kids could pull a cord on the doll's back. This made her say things. Christie was marketed as Barbie's friend.

Christie dolls had brown hair and wore brightly colored clothing.

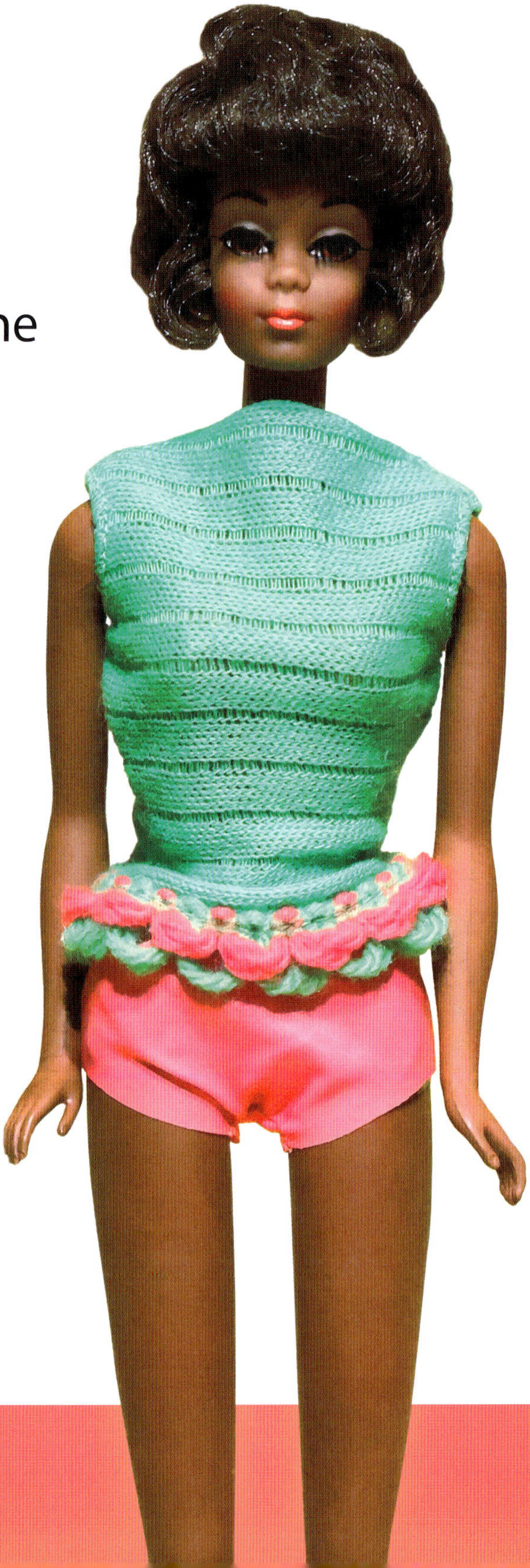

Growing Up Skipper was discontinued in 1977.

Skipper Grows Up

More Skipper dolls came out during the 1970s. One was Growing Up Skipper. This doll was meant to teach kids about growing up. She looked like a regular Skipper. But lifting the doll's arm made her taller. This also made the doll's chest grow. Some people thought that was inappropriate.

A Barbie collector shows off her California Dream Midge doll.

New Characters

In 1987, Mattel launched the California Dream series. It featured Barbie's friends. These included Christie and Midge. The line also introduced a new friend, Teresa. She was Mattel's first Latina doll. Teresa had brown hair and eyes. She wore a yellow polka-dot outfit.

More Sisters

In 1990, Mattel introduced Kelly. She was Barbie and Skipper's little sister. The doll was renamed Stacie in 1992. Then in 1995, Mattel released another Kelly doll. She was the family's youngest sister. Kelly was a baby or toddler in early sets. Later versions were older. Kelly's name changed to Chelsea in 2011.

The Roberts Sisters

Barbie's sisters have changed over the years. Barbie had a baby sister named Krissy at one point. Skipper was redesigned in 2009. She had brown hair with purple streaks.

Chelsea dolls come in different skin colors and have many hairstyles.

Introducing Becky

Share a Smile Becky was the first Barbie in a wheelchair. She came out in 1997. The next year, School Photographer Becky came out. This doll carried a camera. Another Becky was released in 2000. She had a racing wheelchair.

Mattel released three versions of the Becky doll.

Between 2002 and 2005, many playsets were sold under the Happy Family line.

Happy Family

In 2002, Mattel released the Happy Family line. It featured Midge and a doll named Alan. They were married with kids. Midge & Baby was one doll in the line. She had a pregnant belly. The belly could be removed to reveal a baby inside. Some people thought the doll was inappropriate for kids.

Midge and Allan were also featured in the *Barbie* movie. Actor Michael Cera played Allan.

Hi, Barbie!

The Barbies and Kens in the 2023 *Barbie* film live in Barbieland. Actors played different versions of the dolls. Issa Rae was President Barbie. Kate McKinnon was Weird Barbie. Simu Liu also played Ken. The film introduced non-Barbie characters as well. America Ferrera starred as Gloria. She helps save Barbieland.

Cast of Characters

Mattel designed several dolls based on the *Barbie* cast. One was President Barbie. This doll wore a sparkly pink gown. Another doll was Gloria. She wore a pink pantsuit and heels. Mattel also made a doll of Simu Liu's Ken.

In the film, Gloria works at Mattel.

Barbie's First Fashions

In 1959, Mattel released the first Barbie clothing. Charlotte Johnson worked for Mattel. She was a former women's clothing designer. She designed the original Barbie outfits. These included the black-and-white swimsuit. Most Barbie outfits at that time were sold separately from the dolls.

Designer Charlotte Johnson worked at Mattel for more than 20 years.

The Easter Parade outfit included a dress, coat, gloves, and hat.

Original Looks

Twenty-three Barbie clothing sets were originally released. Three sets were sold only in 1959. These were Gay Parisienne, Easter Parade, and Roman Holiday. Continued sets included wedding dresses and evening gowns.

Some 1960s Barbie clothing was based on the style of former First Lady Jackie Kennedy.

1960s Fashions

Throughout the 1960s, Mattel released more clothing sets. They were modeled after popular trends. The 1960 Enchanted Evening set featured a satin gown and fur shawl. Other styles included a tennis outfit and a flight attendant outfit.

Fashion Paks

In 1962, Mattel began offering Fashion Paks. These clothing sets were not full outfits. They came with one item or accessory. This made them cheaper than other sets. Fashion Paks included items such as kitchen aprons and purses. This made it easy for kids to mix and match their Barbies' outfits.

FUN FACT!

Some Fashion Paks came with kitchen tools, such as pots and pans.

Early clothing sets and accessories were sometimes marketed in connection with certain dolls.

1970s Fashions

More clothing sets hit the shelves in the 1970s. These sets represented the decade's bold fashions. Many had bright colors and patterns.

During the 1970s, Mattel partnered with the department store Sears to release exclusive clothing sets.

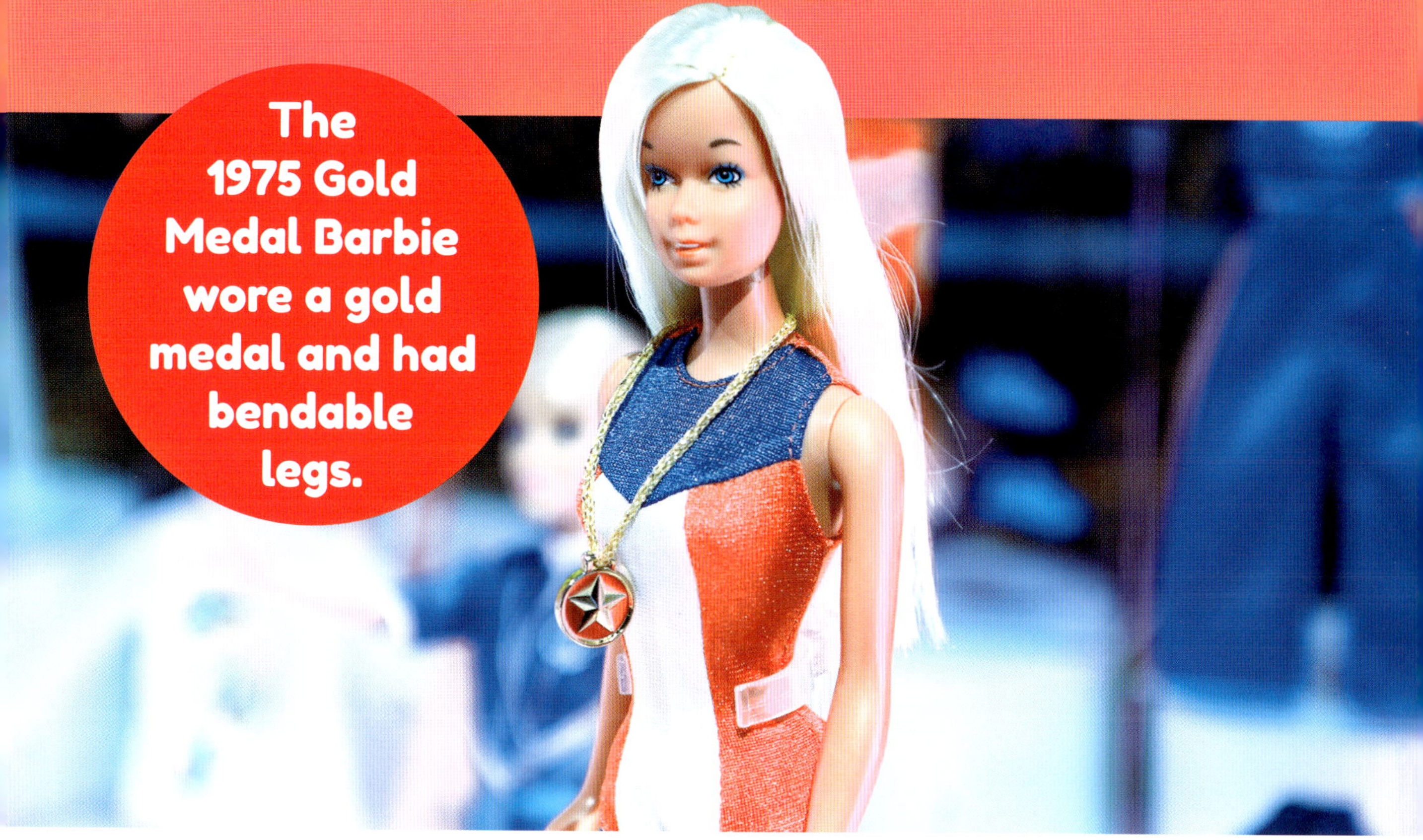

Getting Groovy

In the 1970s, Barbie clothing sets featured many trends. Kids could dress dolls in long dresses and fringed boots. Other sets featured bell-bottom pants. In 1976, the Olympic Games took place. Mattel released Barbie clothing a year before that was inspired by the event.

Gold Medal Barbie

Mattel partnered with the 1976 Olympic Games. It created Gold Medal Barbie dolls and sets. Mattel also released Olympics outfits for Ken.

Some dolls from the 1980s had very bright and bold makeup.

1980s Fashions

Barbie wore new fashion trends in the 1980s. Clothing sets featured puffy sleeves, jeans, and power suits. Barbies also had a variety of dresses. Bright colors and patterns were common.

Totally Trendy

One 1980s Barbie wore a shiny ball gown. It had ruffles and a pink belt. Great Shape Barbie had leg warmers and a bright blue leotard. She came with workout accessories. She also carried a duffel bag. Loving You Barbie wore a red-and-white gown. The gown had hearts printed on it.

Great Shape Barbie released in 1983.

1990s Fashions

The 1990s brought changing fashion trends. Mattel released new clothing sets based on these trends. Many featured casual items. These included jeans, T-shirts, and crop tops. Other sets embraced the glamour of past decades.

Holiday Barbies were a popular collectible series during the 1990s.

The Generation Girl collection included six dolls.

Changing Styles

Some 1990s clothing sets had themed outfits. These included sports uniforms or wedding dresses. One 1993 doll wore an Air Force pilot uniform. In 1998, Mattel launched Generation Girl. This line involved new Barbie characters. It also had unique clothing sets. The fashions could fit all the characters.

Pink is a common color for Barbie clothing.

The 2000s

In the 2000s, Mattel updated Barbie's look again. The Fashion Avenue line offered sets with multiple items. Kids could mix and match the items to create new looks. In 2004, the Fashion Fever line launched. It focused on modern fashions.

Fairy Tale Fashions

During the 2000s, several animated Barbie films came out. Many told stories of princesses and magic. Some featured fairies and mermaids. Mattel released dolls and clothing sets inspired by these movies. Many sets featured gowns seen in the films. Others came with fairy wings.

Mattel made several dolls based on the film *Barbie: Mariposa and the Fairy Princess.*

Barbie Fashions Today

Today, Mattel continues to offer Barbie clothing sets. Kids can collect packs of clothes and accessories. Mattel also sells closet playsets. These include a variety of clothing pieces. They come with accessories such as hangers.

Kids can mix and match Barbie and Ken clothes to create their own looks.

Today, Barbie clothes and accessories are inspired by both new and old fashion trends.

World of Styles

In the 2020s, many clothing sets had themes. One set had a winter theme. It included a snowflake purse and silver shoes. Mattel also offered BarbieStyle fashions. These were exclusive sets. One set featured a blazer and beret. Another included a tennis sweatshirt.

The 1962 Dreamhouse could fold up into a carrying case. This allowed kids to take the house on the go.

First Dreamhouse

In 1962, Mattel released the first Barbie Dreamhouse. It was a cardboard dollhouse. The house had a single room. The room was decorated with pictures and bookshelves. Kids could move cardboard furniture around the room. The set came with a sofa, chair, and bed.

Dreamhouse Details

The 1962 Barbie Dreamhouse came with many decorations. One was a framed photo of Ken. There were also tiny versions of real record albums.

New Home

The Barbie New Dreamhouse came out in 1964. The house was made of cardboard. It had two rooms. It came with furniture such as a TV and nightstand. It also had new features such as a sliding door. In 1965, Mattel changed its Dreamhouse design. It switched to plastic.

Early Barbie houses had closets to hang clothes in.

The first Barbie Townhouse was 3.5 feet (1.1 m) tall.

The Dreamhouse Expands

Most early Barbie houses were single rooms or apartments. But the 1974 Townhouse featured three floors. It also had a yellow elevator. In 1979, Mattel introduced a full-size dollhouse. Openings in the roof allowed kids to access each room. The house also folded open. Kids could rearrange each section.

New Designs

In the 1980s, more Dreamhouses hit the shelves. The Dream Cottage was released in 1982. This was a smaller dollhouse. It had a rooftop patio. Accessories included a grill and an umbrella. The 1983 Townhouse was similar to the 1974 version. But it had a pink elevator.

The 1982 Dream Cottage is considered one of the rarest Barbie houses.

Turning Pink

In 1986, Mattel updated the 1979 Dreamhouse. The new version was painted pink and white. It had a different layout of rooms. The house also had many details. Flower boxes decorated the windows. The windows could open and close.

The 1979 and 1986 Barbie Dreamhouses were shaped in a style known as an A-frame.

The 1990 Magical Mansion had balconies.

Barbie Mansions

Several Dreamhouses released in the 1990s. The 1990 Magical Mansion was pink with lots of decorations. It had floral wallpaper. It also had real lights and a doorbell that rang. Other 1990s Dreamhouses had stained glass windows.

Becky and the Dreamhouse

The 1997 Share a Smile Becky's wheelchair couldn't fit through the Dreamhouse doors. People wrote to Mattel about this. Later, Mattel made the Dreamhouse wheelchair friendly.

Many Barbie houses released during the 2000s, including the Barbie Talking Townhouse.

2000s Dreamhouses

Barbie Dreamhouses continued getting bigger in the 2000s. They became more detailed as well. In 2006 and 2008, Mattel released three-story Dreamhouses. These had spiral staircases. They also had new features such as a washer and dryer. The 2009 Dreamhouse included a hot tub.

Bigger and Better

In 2011, Mattel released the Barbie Malibu Dreamhouse. It had a balcony. The 2016 Hello Dreamhouse was a smart home. Kids could use voice commands to make the house do things. They could use their voice to open doors. And they could turn the stairs into a slide.

People had to download a phone app in order to use the Hello Dreamhouse.

Modern Designs

In the 2020s, Mattel made Dreamhouses more modern. The 2021 Dreamhouse had more than 75 pieces. The furniture could change. The grill could flip to turn into a dessert buffet. Kids could adjust the house's lighting. They could press buttons to play sounds. And the house had a wheelchair lift.

The 2021 Dreamhouse was the first one with a wheelchair lift.

More than 75 accessories and pieces were included in the 2023 Dreamhouse.

Dreamhouses Today

Mattel continues selling Dreamhouses today. In 2023, another Dreamhouse came out. It included ten play spaces. It featured a slide and swimming pool. There were also pet-friendly features. These included a pet slide. The house also had light and sound effects.

Besides salmon pink, the 1962 Austin-Healey car came in red and blue.

First Car

Mattel released the first Barbie car in 1962. It was an Austin-Healey. The car had an open top. It could fit two dolls. The car was sold in several colors. One was salmon pink with blue seats. Another 1962 Barbie car was a Mercedes-Benz. It came in several colors.

Rare Toys

Several Barbie vehicles were made in the 1960s. They included a sports plane, boat, and hot rod car. Today, these toys are rare.

FUN FACT!

Mattel is also the creator of Hot Wheels toy cars.

Barbie Goes Camping

In 1970, Mattel introduced the Country Camper. It had a foldout table and sliding door. The camper also came with accessories. These included a tent and sleeping bags. Several other campers came out during the 1970s. One was the 1976 Star Traveler.

The Country Camper included a small kitchen inside.

Star'Vette

Mattel continued creating new cars for Barbie. In 1976, it introduced the Star'Vette. It was modeled after a Corvette sports car. The Star'Vette came in purple and hot pink. It had stars on it. Mattel released several versions of the car. The 1979 Super'Vette came with a remote control.

The Star'Vette had a luggage rack on the back of it.

The Barbie Ferrari could fit two dolls and included seat belts.

1980s Cars

Mattel created many Barbie vehicles during the 1980s. These included horse trailers, jeeps, and race cars. There was even a dune buggy. In 1987, Mattel released a Barbie Ferrari. This car came in red and white.

Beetles and Mini Vans

The 2002 Volkswagen Microbus came in several colors, including pink and purple.

In 1995, Mattel released the Barbie Mini Van. Dolls could sit in the front or back seats. There were even seat belts.

In 2000, Mattel partnered with the car company Volkswagen. They created the Barbie Volkswagen Beetle. Kids could decorate it with stickers.

Cool Campers

In 2015, a Barbie pop-up camper came out. It was based on the animated film *Barbie & Her Sisters in the Great Puppy Adventure*. The pink camper had three levels. It included a kitchen, bathroom, and beds. Two years later, the Barbie DreamCamper released. It had hammocks and a waterslide.

A bathroom and kitchen were featured inside the 2017 Barbie DreamCamper.

Off-Road Vehicles

In the 2020s, Mattel released several Barbie vehicles. Some were off-road vehicles. One 2020 release was purple with pink seats. It had an open top. Two dolls could fit in the car. The car also had seat belts.

Barbie car wheels roll to allow kids to easily move the cars around.

People can take the top off the Barbie electric car to turn it into a convertible.

New Features

Some modern Barbie vehicles had new features. In 2021, a pink Barbie car came out. It was based on the animated film *Barbie: Big City, Big Dreams*. The car's roof could turn into a music stage. In 2022, an electric Barbie car was released. It came with a charging station.

The Barbie Dreamplane could fit three dolls inside.

Dreamplane

In 2019, a Barbie Dreamplane hit the shelves. This pink plane opened to reveal seats. The seats could recline. It had a seat for the pilot too. The set came with more than 15 accessories. These included snack carts, headphones, and luggage.

Pink Convertibles

In the 2020s, Mattel released several Barbie convertibles. Many came in pink. Some were remote-controlled. One 2020 convertible featured sparkly pink paint. The dashboard included a sticker of a map screen. Kids could fit two dolls into the cars.

Barbie vehicles are sold in toy stores around the world.

DreamCamper

The Barbie 3-in-1 DreamCamper released in 2020. The front of the vehicle could turn into a pickup truck. A boat could be stored under the back seat. The camper also had a kitchen, living room, and bathroom.

FUN FACT!

The DreamCamper came with 60 accessories, including fishing poles and cooking tools.

The DreamCamper could hold up to four dolls.

The Corvette from *Barbie* was based on real cars from the 1950s.

Classic Corvette

In the 2023 *Barbie* film, Barbie drives a pink Corvette convertible. Mattel made several toy versions of this car. The car had a pink steering wheel. Four dolls could fit inside it. Mattel also offered a remote-controlled convertible. This car could fit two dolls. Its trunk opened and closed.

In 2001, Mattel sold a Sugarplum Princess doll that could do ballet.

The Nutcracker

In 2001, Mattel released its first animated Barbie movie. It was *Barbie in the Nutcracker*. The film featured music from a ballet. In the film, Barbie plays Clara. She helps a nutcracker defeat a mouse king. Mattel released several dolls based on the film.

Barbie's Voice

Kelly Sheridan is a voice actress. She voiced Barbie in many animated films. She played the character throughout the 2000s.

Rapunzel

Barbie as Rapunzel came out in 2002. It was based on a fairy tale. In the story, a witch locks Rapunzel in a tower. Rapunzel falls in love with a prince. He helps her escape from the tower. Several Barbie Rapunzel dolls were made. One had special hair. It could be made shorter or longer.

Kids could brush the Barbie Rapunzel doll's hair.

Swan Lake

Barbie of Swan Lake released in 2003. The movie was based on a ballet. Barbie starred as Odette. An evil wizard turns her into a swan. Odette must save the Enchanted Forest from the wizard. Mattel sold Odette dolls in different outfits. People could also buy a carriage and castle.

The Odette doll had wings that could light up.

People could push a button on the Erika and Princess Anneliese dolls to make them sing.

Princess and the Pauper

Barbie as the Princess and the Pauper came out in 2004. This was the first Barbie musical. In it, Princess Anneliese meets a girl named Erika. They look alike. The girls switch places to save the kingdom. Mattel sold Anneliese and Erika dolls.

Original Songs

Barbie as the Princess and the Pauper features seven original songs. One is "I Am a Girl Like You." Another is "To Be a Princess."

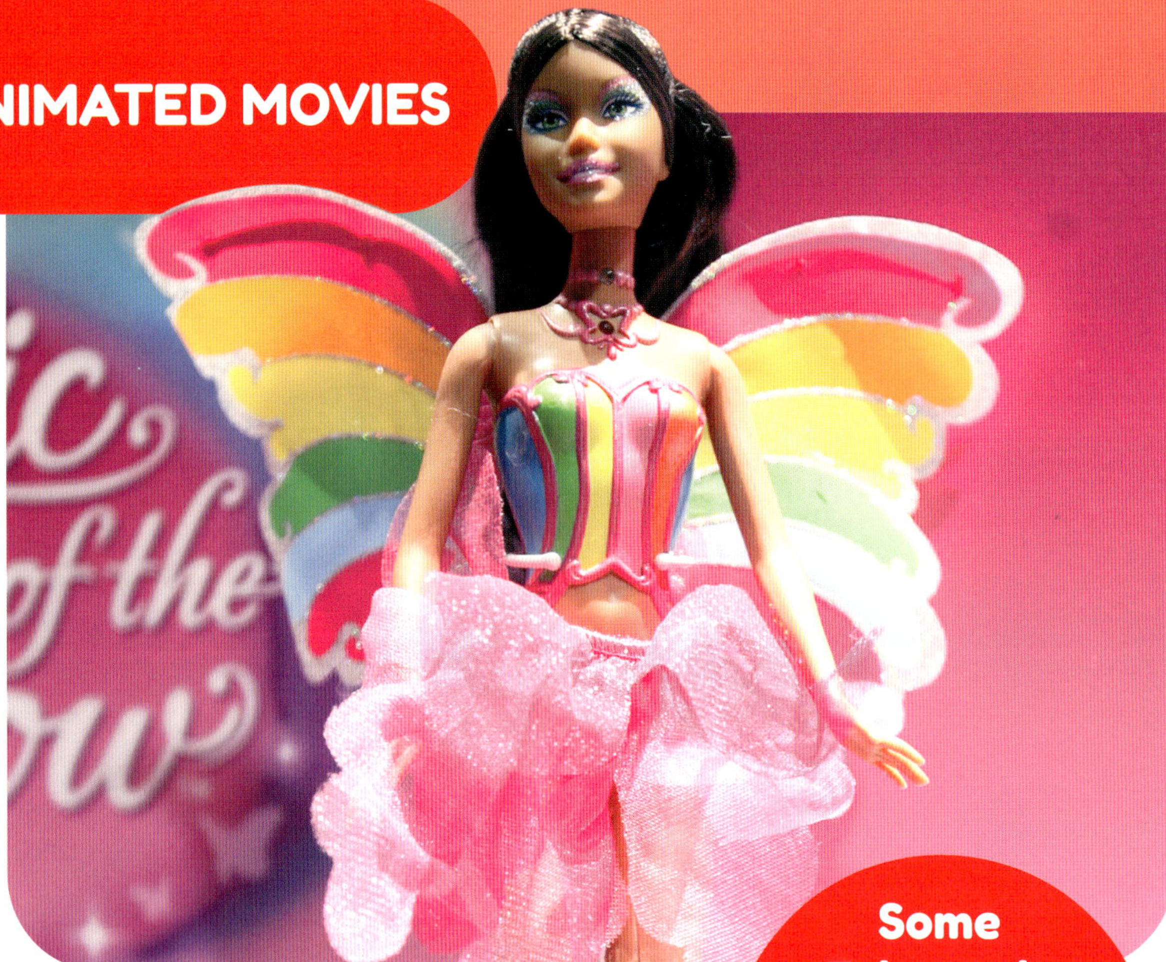

Some Fairytopia dolls had rainbow-colored wings and outfits.

Fairytopia

In 2005, *Barbie: Fairytopia* was released. Barbie played Elina. She is a fairy without wings. She must save Fairytopia. Mattel sold several dolls inspired by the movie. They had colorful hair and wings. Mini playsets were also available. They featured places from the movie.

The Story Continues

Mattel released more Fairytopia movies. In 2006, *Barbie Fairytopia: Mermaidia* came out. In it, Elina must rescue a merman prince. Dolls with mermaid tails were sold. *Barbie Fairytopia: Magic of the Rainbow* released in 2007. Elina goes to Fairy School in this film.

Spin-Offs

Two Barbie films were Fairytopia spin-offs. These were *Barbie: Mariposa* and *Barbie: Mariposa and the Fairy Princess.*

One Elina doll had fairy wings that transformed into a mermaid tail.

Magic of Pegasus

Barbie and the Magic of Pegasus came out in 2005. Barbie plays Princess Annika. Annika meets her long-lost sister, Brietta. Brietta was turned into a Pegasus. The sisters work together to save the kingdom. Mattel sold Pegasus playsets based on the movie.

The 2005 Princess Annika doll came with a light-up wand.

Mattel sold many toys based on *Barbie in the 12 Dancing Princesses.* These included dolls, playsets, and styling heads.

Twelve Dancing Princesses

In 2006, Mattel released *Barbie in the 12 Dancing Princesses*. Barbie plays Princess Genevieve. She and her sisters discover a magical land. It appears when they dance. Dolls of all 12 sisters were sold.

The *Barbie: A Fashion Fairytale* castle playset released in 2010.

Modern Fairy Tales

Barbie: A Fashion Fairytale released in 2010. In this movie, Barbie goes to Paris, France. She works with fairies. They must save her aunt's fashion business. In 2011, *Barbie: Princess Charm School* came out. It features Barbie as Blair. She attends princess school. Mattel sold fashion packs inspired by these films.

FUN FACT!

A web series called *Barbie: Life in the Dreamhouse* ran from 2012 until 2015.

Changing Themes

In 2015, Mattel released Barbie films with new stories. One was *Barbie in Rock 'n Royals*. Barbie stars as Princess Courtney. She switches places with a rock star. Another film was *Barbie in Princess Power*. In it, Barbie is a princess who has superpowers.

Mattel sold dolls of Corinne, who was a character in *Barbie in Princess Power*.

Magic and Music

In 2017, Mattel released *Barbie: Dolphin Magic*. In the film, Barbie and her sisters go to an island. They meet a magical dolphin and mermaid. *Barbie: Big City, Big Dreams* came out in 2021. In this movie, Barbie attends music school.

In 2021, a *Barbie: Big City, Big Dreams* car playset was released. The car's roof turned into a stage.

Skipper sets feature her doing many jobs, such as babysitting, walking dogs, and working at a snack bar.

New Adventures

Barbie and Chelsea: The Lost Birthday came out in 2022. This was the first movie to star Chelsea. In it, Chelsea's birthday gets erased. She must save it. In 2023, *Barbie: Skipper and the Big Babysitting Adventure* was released. Mattel sold dolls inspired by these films.

Along with hair accessories, some styling heads came with jewelry, including rings, necklaces, and bracelets.

Styling Heads

Mattel makes more than just Barbie dolls and dreamhouses. There are many other Barbie toys. Styling heads are large Barbie heads. They have long, soft hair. Kids can style the hair. The sets often come with accessories. These include combs and hair clips.

Then and Now

The first Barbie styling heads came out in the 1970s. They featured a blonde Barbie. Accessories included curlers and a comb. Later, Mattel updated the design of its styling heads. It made them more diverse. Some came with accessories such as hair extensions.

Styling heads today often come with colorful hair.

Mini BarbieLand

In 2024, Mattel launched the Mini BarbieLand line. It featured mini dolls and playsets. Some are based on full-size Barbies such as the Cutie Reveal dolls. Others feature Fashionistas dolls. They are packaged inside lipstick tubes. There are also Mini BarbieLand cars, planes, and houses.

The Mini BarbieLand Doll House set includes a slide and a working elevator.

The Mega Bloks Barbie Build 'n Play Glam Salon set released in 2013.

Mega Sets

Mattel started releasing Barbie Mega Bloks sets in the 2010s. Mega Bloks are like Legos. Kids can build versions of popular Barbie playsets. One set came with a pink convertible and ice cream stand. The Dreamhouse from the 2023 *Barbie* movie is another set. It comes with mini dolls and furniture pieces.

GLOSSARY

accessible
Designed to be usable for people with disabilities.

accessory
An additional object or item that comes with a toy or playset.

beauty standards
A set of ideas about what is and isn't beautiful.

debut
To make a first appearance.

discontinue
To stop producing or selling.

diverse
Representing many different kinds of people.

inclusive
Welcoming to and accepting of all types of people.

market
To sell or advertise in a specific way.

partnered
Worked together.

pauper
A poor person.

prosthetic
A human-made limb, such as an arm or leg.

rare
Not occurring often.

represent
To be an example or model of something.

theme
The main story or subject.

TO LEARN MORE

More Books to Read

Easton, Marilyn. *Barbie Collector's Guide*. Studio Fun International, 2022.

Hansen, Grace. *Barbie*. Abdo, 2023.

Slater, Lee. *Barbie: Ruth Handler*. Abdo, 2022.

Online Resources

Booklinks
NONFICTION NETWORK
FREE! ONLINE NONFICTION RESOURCES

To learn more about Barbie, please visit **abdobooklinks.com** or scan this QR code. These links are routinely monitored and updated to provide the most current information available.

INDEX

PHOTO CREDITS

Cover Photos: Chesnot/Getty Images Entertainment/Getty Images, front (original Barbie); Mattel/Mega/IBLIM/Newscom, front (President Barbie); Adobe Stock, front (car); Lawrence Lucier/Getty Images Entertainment/Getty Images, front (house); Ina Fassbender/AFP/Getty Images, back

Interior Photos: Daniel Karmann/dpa/picture alliance/Getty Images, 1, 61, 96; Shutterstock Images, 3, 4, 5, 7, 8 (bottom), 20 (left), 26, 30 (bottom), 34, 35, 44, 45, 48 (left), 48 (right), 49, 50, 62 (top), 69 (top), 79 (top), 79 (bottom), 80, 88 (bottom), 89, 93 (bottom), 98 (top), 98 (bottom), 106, 108, 110 (bottom), 113 (bottom), 115 (top), 119, 121, 123; AP Images, 6, 8 (top); Gabe Ginsberg/Getty Images for Barbie: A Cultural Icon Exhibition/Getty Images Entertainment/Getty Images, 9, 16, 88 (top); Hulton Archive/Getty Images, 10, 55; Matthieu Alexandre/AFP/Getty Images, 11; Frederic Reglain/Alamy, 12; Red Line Editorial, 13, 52, 124; Frederic Neema/Sygma/Getty Images, 14; Abdo Publishing, 15, 23; Peter Bischoff/PB Archive/Getty Images, 17, 76; Lawrence Lucier/Getty Images Entertainment/Getty Images, 18, 71, 94, 102, 112; Eduardo Parra/Getty Images Entertainment/Getty Images, 19; Alessandra Tarantino/AP Images, 20 (right); Gabriel Bouys/AFP/Getty Images, 21, 78; Roberto Serra/Iguana Press/Getty Images Entertainment/Getty Images, 22; Jacquelyn Martin/AP Images, 24; Borna Filic/Pixsell/Alamy, 25; Luca Bruno/AP Images, 27; Benjamin Cremel/AFP/Getty Images, 28; Mattel/SIPA/Newscom, 29; Courtesy of The Strong National Museum of Play, Rochester, New York, USA, 30 (top), 91, 125; Yvonne Hemsey/Hulton Archive/Getty Images, 31, 70; Andre Chung/The Washington Post/Getty Images, 32; Wiktor Szymanowicz/Future Publishing/Getty Images, 33; Craig Barritt/Getty Images for Glamour/Getty Images Entertainment/Getty Images, 36; Diane Bondareff/Invision for Barbie/AP Images, 37; Diane Bondareff/AP Images for Mattel/Invision/AP Images, 38; Ina Fassbender/AFP/Getty Images, 39; Christoph Schmidt/dpa/picture alliance/Getty Images, 40; Manoli Figetakis/Getty Images Entertainment/Getty Images, 41, 66, 73; Kristy Sparow/Getty Images Entertainment/Getty Images, 42; Patti McConville/Alamy, 43, 104, 120; Warner Bros./Photofest, 46, 62 (bottom); Cover Images/ZumaPress/Newscom, 47; Mattel Inc./Mega/IBLIM/Newscom, 51; James Manning/PA Images/Getty Images, 53; Mattel/Newsmakers/Hulton Archive/Getty Images, 54, 58; Christof Stache/AFP/Getty Images, 56; Rasid Necati Aslim/Anadolu/Getty Images, 57, 99; Dima Gavrysh/AP Images, 59; Mandel Ngan/AFP/Getty Images, 60; Matt Hunt/Anadolu Agency/Getty Images, 63; Malcolm Park/Alamy Live News/Alamy, 64, 92; Alessandra Schellnegger/Sueddeutsche Zeitung Photo/Alamy, 65 (box); Teenage Doll/Alamy, 65 (doll); Simon Isabelle/Sipa/AP Images, 67; Emily Schwarze/The Houma Courier/AP Images, 68; Jakub Porzycki/NurPhoto/Getty Images, 69 (bottom), 107; Warner Bros./Album/Alamy, 72; Tony Korody/Sygma/Getty Images, 74; Chesnot/Getty Images Entertainment/Getty Images, 75, 87; Brittany Murray/MediaNews Group/Long Beach Press-Telegram/Getty Images, 77; Universal History Archive/Universal Images Group/Getty Images, 81; Richard Lautens/Toronto Star/Getty Images, 82; Marty Lederhandler/AP Images, 83; STR/AFP/Getty Images, 84; Daniel Karmann/picture alliance/Getty Images, 85; Anthony Behar/Sipa USA/AP Images, 86; Ed Maker/Denver Post/Getty Images, 90; Charlie J. Ercilla/Alamy, 93 (top); Mark Lennihan/AP Images, 95; Kazuki Oishi/Sipa USA/AP Images, 97; John Dooley/Sipa Press/Newscom, 100; Matt Rittle/Mirrorpix/Getty Images, 101; Diane Bondareff/AP Images for Mattel/AP Images, 103; David Benito/Getty Images Entertainment/Getty Images, 105; Rodin Eckenroth/FilmMagic/Getty Images, 109; Mattel/Getty Images Entertainment/Getty Images, 110 (top); Ian West/PA Images/Getty Images, 111; Richard Drew/AP Images, 113 (top); Jason Merritt/FilmMagic for Ketchum Entertainment Marketing/Getty Images, 114; Joe Raedle/Getty Images News/Getty Images, 115 (bottom); Matt Faber/PA Images/Getty Images, 116; Nick Ut/AP Images, 117; Reed Saxon/AP Images, 118; Emmanuel Dunand/AFP/Getty Images, 122